DELUXE ILLUSTRATED LYRICS BOOK

of THE UNPREDICTABLE ROCK-AND-ROLL JOURNEY

Please print passenger name on ticket.

NAME OF PASSENGER/NOM DU PASSAGER:

FROM/DE:
NRTHEAST STA
TO/A:
NOWHERE
TRAIN
54

ISSUE DATE
3APR09

TIME/L'HEURE DU DEPART:
12.00/MIDNIGHT

FARE/TARIF N/A
MULTI TRIP

RIDE# 1 2 3 4 5 6 7 8

GOOD FOR PASSAGE

MUSIC *by* SANDRA BOYNTON & MICHAEL FORD

LYRICS *and* DRAWINGS *by* SANDRA BOYNTON

WORKMAN PUBLISHING • NEW YORK

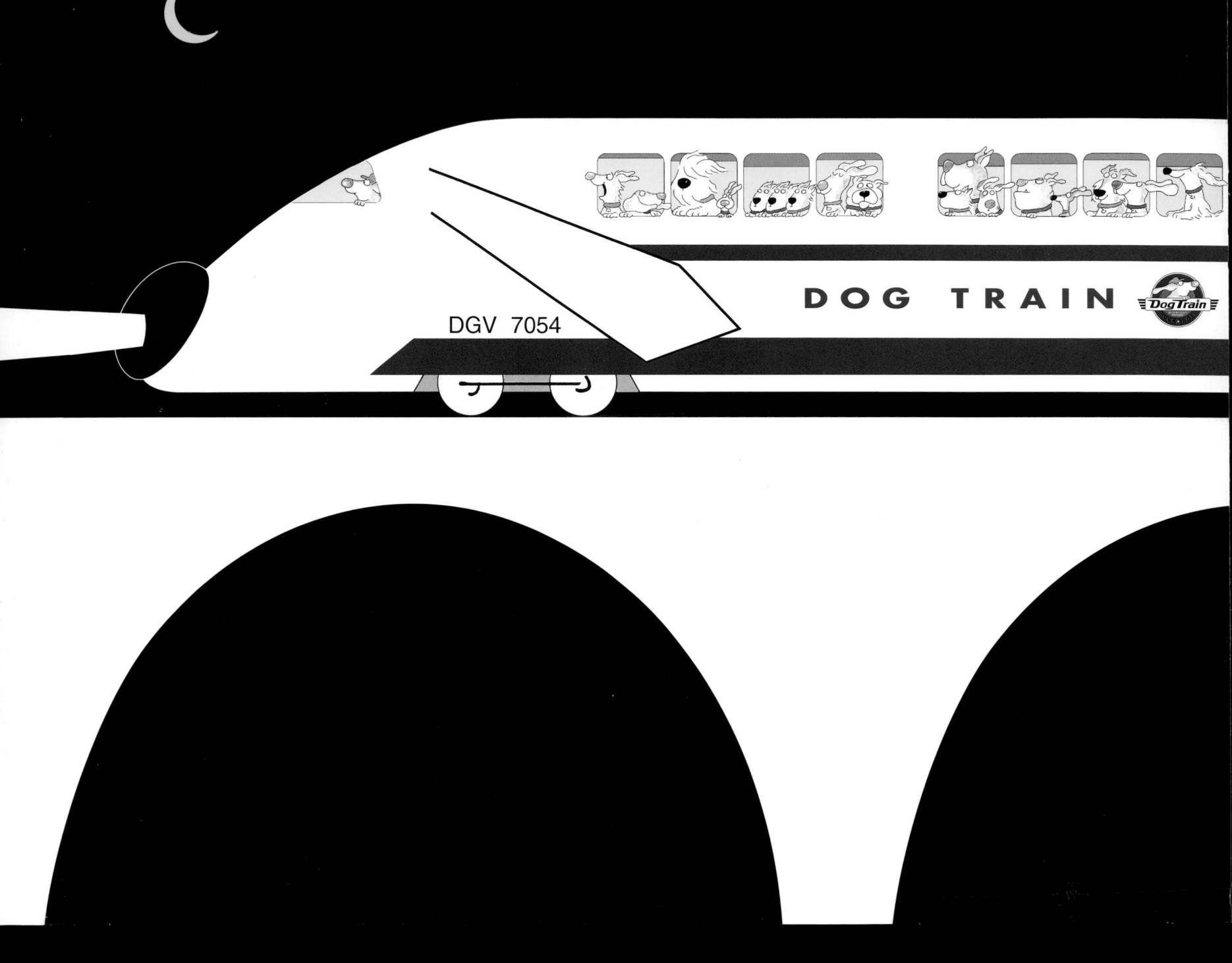

DogTrain

MIDNIGHT EXPRESS

7054

To all of the terrific children (some of them furry) of the entire Dog Train crew—

CAITLIN, KEITH, DEVIN, DARCY, RACHEL, JOHN, KATIE,
ZEPHYR, GILLIGAN, ZOË, TIPPY, FANG, BETSY, BRINDLE,
CHRISTIAN, SPENCER, THISTLE, LADY, VENUS, DUKE, SPIRIT, ARIES,
SAMANTHA, WYLLIE, RUBY, DAVID, AYDEN, ROWAN,
ANNABELLE, JOSEPHINE, DOMINIC, BARNABY, RUPERT, BERNADETTE,
MABEL, NEAL, TRAVIS, SOSIE, NINA, MIA, JOE, LILLIAN, SAM,
AUBRI, ASHA, ETHAN, ERICA, JOHNNY, OLIVIA, ORBIT,
CARY, MARLEE, KENNY, MADELYNN, DANIELLA, CAMERON, REESA, MADDIE,
ROLLY, MASON, AILEY, GRACIE, EMMA, SIMON, MAIA, FRODE,
MATTHEW, NICHOLAS, TADDY AND FADDY (FROGS),
AUSTIN, ANDREW, ALEX, ADEN, KARI, KATIE, KRISTIE, RYAN, PEPPER,
CHRIS, TOMMY, LUCIE, KACIE, ZOË, JULIANNA, CATHERINE,
ALICE, NED, KATIE, ELIZABETH, JACK & MADELINE

Boring Song & Evermore ©Boynton/Ford Music (ASCAP)   All other songs ©SKBoynton Music (ASCAP)

Library of Congress Cataloging-in-Publication Data is available.

WORKMAN PUBLISHING COMPANY, INC., 225 VARICK STREET, NEW YORK, NY 10014-4381 WWW.WORKMAN.COM WWW.SANDRABOYNTON.COM
PRINTED IN CHINA. FIRST PRINTING: OCTOBER 2005

PART ONE

LOOK AS YOU LISTEN

Tantrum

No—I don't want to. I don't want to.
No—I don't want to. No no.
No—I don't want to. I don't want to.
No, no, no. I don't want to. Oh no.
Leave me...alone.

I don't want to be quiet. I don't want to be good.
I don't want to do anything if you tell me I should.
I won't listen to you. If you call, I won't come.
All I want to do now...

[kindly turn the page]

NO NO NO, I DON'T WANT TO, I DON'T WANT TO. NO NO NO, I DON'T WANT TO, NO NO.

Tantrum

...is have a tantrum.

**NO NO NO,
I DON'T WANT TO. I DON'T WANT TO.
NO NO NO.
I DON'T WANT TO. NO NO.**

**NO NO NO,
I DON'T WANT TO. I DON'T WANT TO.
NO NO NO.
I DON'T WANT TO. NO NO.**

**NO NO NO,
I DON'T WANT TO. I DON'T WANT TO.
NO NO NO.
I DON'T WANT TO. NO NO.**

LEAVE ME ALONE. LEAVE ME ALONE.

LEAVE ME ALONE!

FOR MUSIC AND ALL LYRICS,
PLEASE TURN TO PAGE 40

THE O.K. CHORALE

TRACK # 2 Thus Quacked Zarathustra

Mooooooooo…Mooooooooo…Mooooooooo…

QUACK-QUACK!

Dog Train

Along about midnight when it's dark, dark, dark,
there's a long, low whistle and a faraway bark,
and then a high, high whistle only hounds can hear
to let 'em know the train, the Dog Train, is near.

DGV 7054

*Dog Train! Riding all night long, on that
Dog Train! They'll be riding till dawn.
You'll never ever see it as it rockets past—
The train goes nowhere, but it goes there fast.
Dog Train.*

DOG TRAIN

FOR MUSIC & ALL LYRICS,
PLEASE TURN TO PAGE 42

When you're unaware that a bear is there, well, here's the reason why: it's the SNEAKERS.
Now you know.

TRACK #
4

Sneakers

Well, I'm a big ol' bear, and I don't wear much of anything, 'cause I've got fur.
But these big ol' feet wouldn't be complete without my shoes. No sir.
I'm talkin' about
S N E A K E R S . *Yeah.*

My old sneakers are friends of mine—
You can't trust any shoes that shine.
Some shoes pinch you, some shoes squeak.
The only shoes that I would choose are shoes that sneak.
I'm telling you, my old sneakers are friends of mine—
You can't trust any shoes that shine.
Some shoes pinch you, some shoes squeak.
The only shoes that I would choose are shoes that sneak.

Whoa! Look at these guys!

Well, there's a toe that is torn and the laces are worn
so I've added a section of string.
I'm not even sure what color they were,
but now they're a little of everything.

FOR MUSIC & ALL LYRICS,
PLEASE TURN TO PAGE 43

And we'll keep on rock-and-rolling through outer space till we find find find that magical place.
Cow Planet. Ohhhhh! Cow Planet.

TRACK #

5

Cow Planet

Another time. Another place. Somewhere far... out in space.
Listen:

"COWWWWWWW PLANET. AH–OOM..."

Who they are, we don't know. Now they call. We must go. Cow Planet.

We're gonna go fast and we're gonna go far
with a steady-driving bass and a rhythm guitar.
We've got a blazing afterburner—
it's a backbeat drum.
Get ready, Cow Planet, now, here we come.

Cow Planet.
Hey hey, Cow Planet.
We're really on our way
to Cow Planet.

FOR MUSIC & ALL LYRICS, PLEASE TURN TO PAGE 44

♪ "Won't you let me be boring, so boring for you?" ♪

TRACK #
6

Boring Song

...SUDDENLY HERE YOU ARE

Right in the middle of a boring song.

Boring song!

This song is so boring
and I'm boring, too.
Won't you let me be boring
so boring for you?

Boring wah-oo!

Boring!

*For you-oo-oo,
and tho—*

And though you **FIND** me
boring
still **I'M** adoring
my voice.
I've no choice.

I find you boring!

Boring!

What else can you do?

Yes, what else can I do?
It's impossibly true—
I'd give all that I've got just to tell of
my love for...
ME.

*Boringboringboringboring.
Bo-ring, ooo!*

FOR MUSIC,
PLEASE TURN TO PAGE 45

I'm so happy in the middle of the kitchen floor with whatever I find behind the cabinet door.

TRACK #
7

Pots and Pans

Here we go—

I've got ONE pot.
A metal spoon.
What've you got?
You've got a rhythm tune.
You've got a pot. Spoon.
Rhythm tune.
You've got a pot
AND spoon
AND rhythm tune.
You've got a little, got a lot,
got a musical pot.
Now what? Now what?

I've got pots: Pots and pans.
I've got pots: Pots and pans.
Yeah, that's the way
that I like to play—
banging on pots and pans.
Yeah, banging on pots and pans.

Now another pot.
A wooden spoon.
What've you got?
You've got a rhythm tune.
You've got a pot pot,
spoon spoon, rhythm tune.
You've got a 2-pot
2-spoon 2-2-tune.
You've got a little, got a lot,
you've got whatever you got.
Why not? Oh, yeah, why not?

I've got pots: Pots and pans.
I've got pots: Pots and pans.
Yeah, that's the way
that I like to play—
banging on pots and pans.
Clanging those pots and pans.

FOR MUSIC & ALL LYRICS,
PLEASE TURN TO PAGE 46

♪ *"No more running around—I just need to lie down and sleeeeeep!"* ♪

TRACK #
8

I Need A Nap

Well, the sun is still high in the afternoon sky,
but the morning seems so long ago.
I was happy before and I'm not any more,
though why there's a change, I don't know.

I'm so tired of this day and I don't want to play
and I don't want a story to read.
But I look in your eyes and at once realize
that I know what it is... yes, I know what it is...
now I know what it is that I need—

I NEED A NAP!

I just can't take any more.

I NEED A NAP!

Can't stay awake any more.
No more running around—
I just need to lie down
and sleeeeeep!

STORIES

FOR MUSIC & ALL LYRICS,
PLEASE TURN TO PAGE 47

Evermore I will love you. You're ever my own.

TRACK # 9

Evermore

The forests of April awaken from sleep,
and flowers unfold through the snow,
and the wind rushes high,
and the river runs deep,
and it sings what you already know.
You already know—

*Evermore I will love you,
evermore I will stay
ever right here to hold you.
Never so far away.
And though I know sometimes you go
to find your way alone,
evermore I will love you.
You're ever my own.*

FOR MUSIC & ALL LYRICS,
PLEASE TURN TO PAGE 48

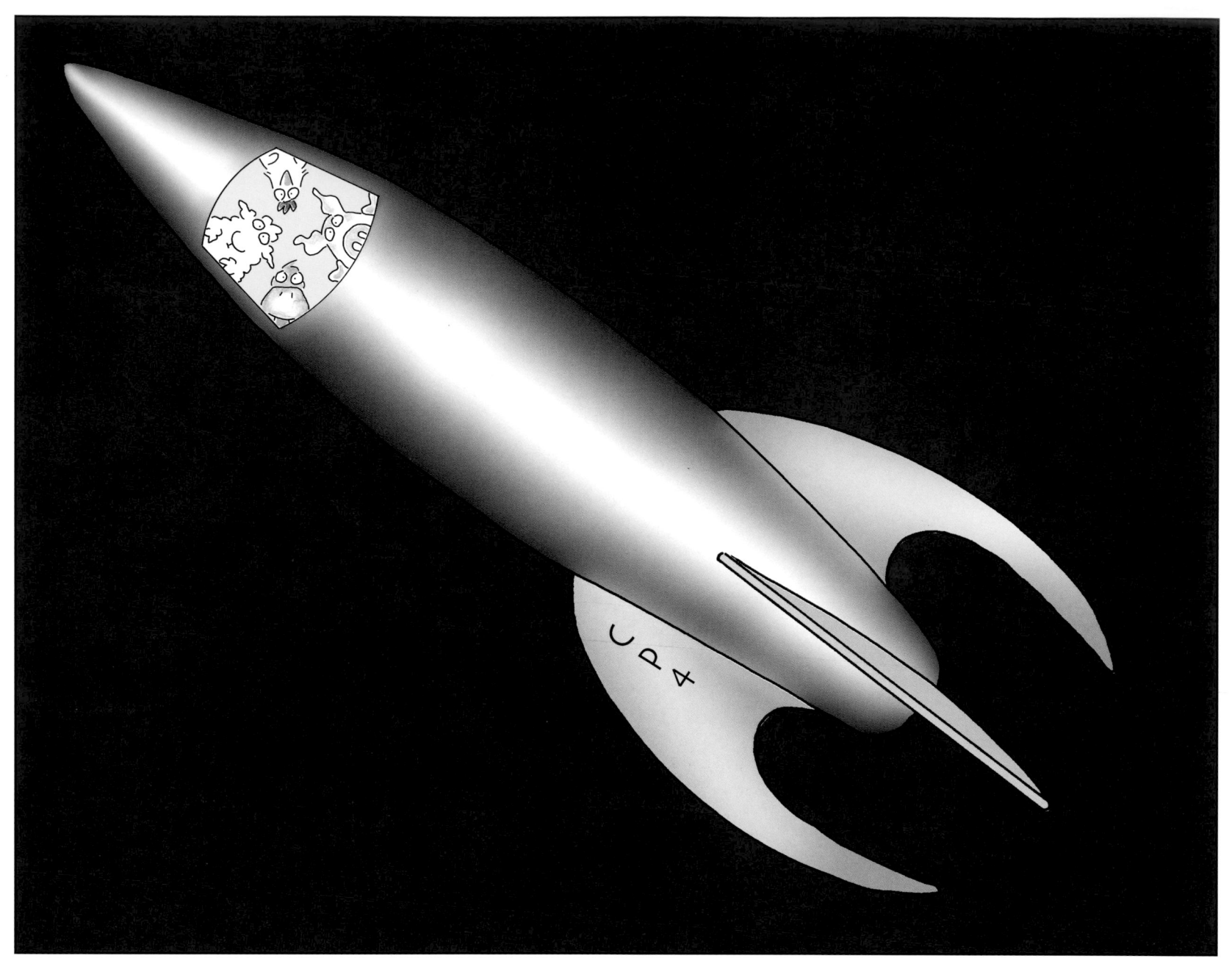

Where oh where is Cow Planet? We really cannot find Cow Planet.

Cow Planet, Episode 2

**Space: Bigger than you can imagine.
The journey continues ...**

Now it's ten years later, and we're still not there,
and we're getting kind of tired of getting nowhere.
We've got a blazing afterburner—
it's an irritating drum—
Get ready, Cow Planet, now, here we come.

*Cow Planet.
Where oh where is Cow Planet?
We really cannot find Cow Planet.
We really really really really really cannot find
Cow Planet.*

Will we find it — or not? Tune in next time.

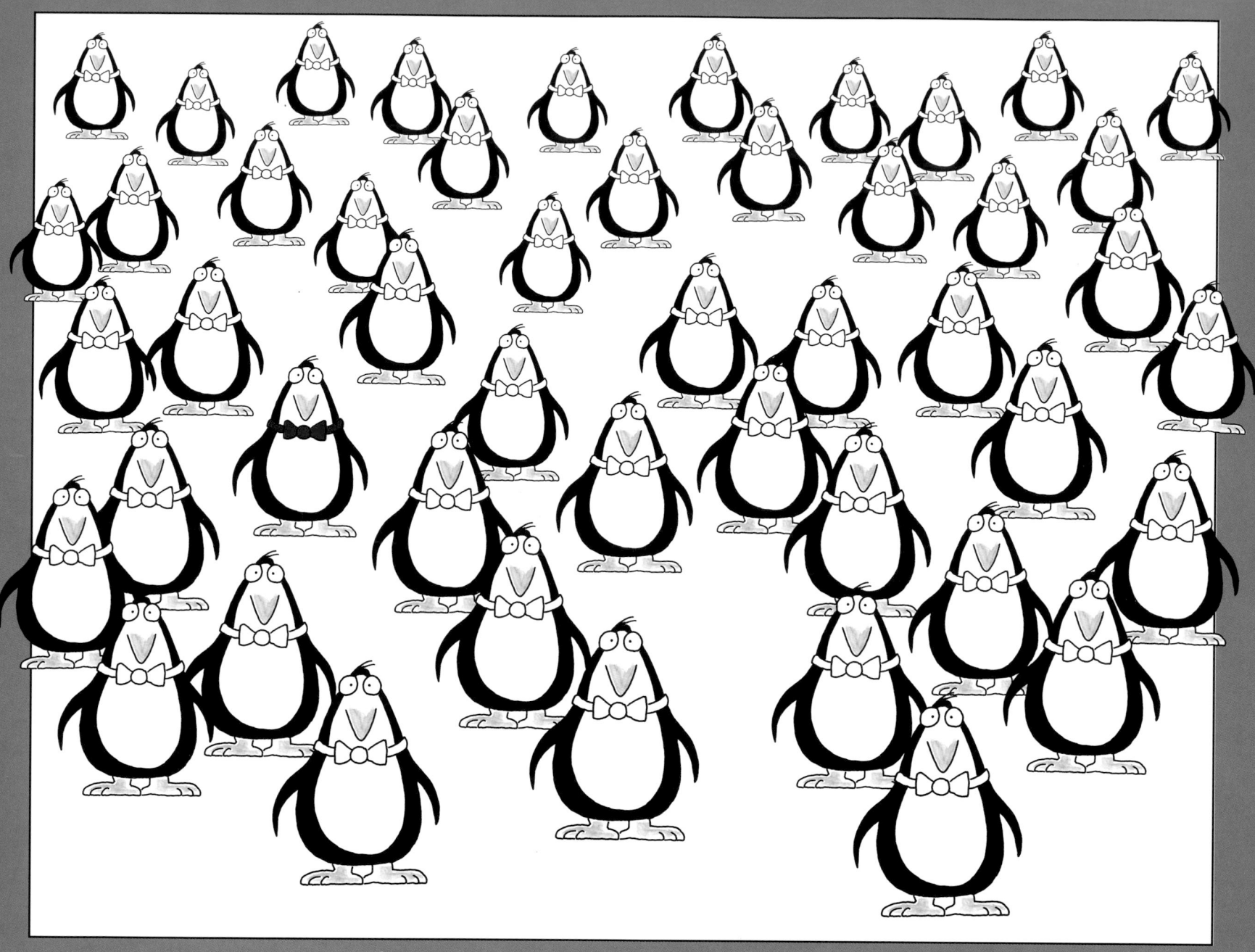

*When you are a penguin, you look around
and see nothing but penguins and frozen ground.*

Penguin Lament

If you were a penguin,
you'd understand
how it is to be a penguin.
It's not always grand.
If you were a penguin,
then you could tell
what it's like to be a penguin.
You'd know too well.

And I'm a little too cute.
Oh, yes, I know.
I'm all dressed up,
but I've got no place to go.

When you are a penguin,
you look around
and see nothing but penguins
and frozen ground.
When you are a penguin
(and I am one)
you have nowhere to hide.
You have no way to run—

Little legs cannot stride
so we rock side to side,
side to side, side to side
to move.

We can't even fly!

And I'm a little too cute.
Oh, yes, I know.
I'm all dressed up,
but I've got no place to go—

I want to be cool,
like the polar bear guys.
I want to be tall
and somewhat mysterious.
But nothing profound
comes in penguin size.
Can anyone small...
be anyone serious?

I'M SERIOUS!

FOR MUSIC & ALL LYRICS,
PLEASE TURN TO PAGE 49

Yes, I know I've never tried it, but it doesn't look right. I want no broccoli tonight.

(Don't Give Me That)
Broccoli

Do-on't give me that broccoLEE. Uh-oh-oh.
Do-on't give me that BROCColi.
Yes, I know I've never tried it, but it doesn't look right.
I want no brocc'li tonight.

Now listen, Nice Lady, I don't want to be unfair,
and I know you try to do your best.
I appreciate the fact that you really do care,
but I have a most important request.
Please listen, can you listen,
won't you listen to me?
I'd rather that you never give me…BROCcoLEE.
Please. Don't don't give me any BROCColi.

Do-on't give me that broccoLEE. Uh-oh-oh.
Do-on't give me that BROCColi.
You tell me it can't hurt me to take one little bite,
but I'm taking no chances tonight.

FOR MUSIC & ALL LYRICS,
PLEASE TURN TO PAGE 50

Dragonfire. It burns so hot, it burns so bright. Dragonfire.

Dragonfire

Dragonfire. It burns so hot,
it burns so bright. Dragonfire.
Dragonfire. It burns so bright,
it burns so very hot.
Dragonfire.

So small I am,
so newly made.
Within me, a flame
to keep me
unafraid.
Unafraid—my Dragonfire.

Dragonfire.
It burns so hot,
it burns so bright. Dragonfire.
Dragonfire. It burns so bright,
it burns so very hot. Dragonfire.

FOR MUSIC & ALL LYRICS, PLEASE TURN TO PAGE 51

TRACK # 14

Cow Planet, Episode 3

Space and more space. And then one day—there it is. Up ahead: Cow Planet.

LANDING IN THREE SECONDS . . . PLANETFALL.

We've arrived.

The rocket door now opens wide. The time has come. We step outside...

COW PLANET

COW PLANET

COW PLANET

COW PLANET

Standing in the bright Cow Planet sunlight, our brave and noble band
is greeted by so many happy cows! And the rest—is History.

YEAAAAAH! PINK COWS! GREEN COWS! BABY BLUE!
O, FANTASTICAL COWS,
LET ME HEAR YOU SAY, "MOO!"

Come on and say bye-bye. I want to go bye-bye. It's time to WAVE! BYE! BYE!

Wave Bye-Bye

Excuse me, please…Mommy?…Excuse me, please…I want to go.

Well, hey hey, pretty Mommy, can you hear me at all?
There's lots of noisy people and they're way too tall.
I don't want to hear that music. I don't like the food.
It's enough to put a child in a very bad mood.

Come on and say bye-bye.
I want to go bye-bye.
It's time to wave bye-bye.
Wave bye-bye.

There's a lot of conversation going on and on.
If we never get going, then we won't be gone.
They said it was a party, but they made a mistake.
How can it be a party, when there isn't a cake? (Yeah.)

Come on and say bye-bye.
I want to go bye-bye.
It's time to wave bye-bye.
Wave bye-bye.

FOR MUSIC & ALL LYRICS,
PLEASE TURN TO PAGE 52

♪ *"I'm gonna rock you—rock you to sleep. I'm gonna rock you, rock you—rock you to sleep."* ♪

Rock to Sleep 54

Oh, little child, won't you settle *DOWN*?
Oh, little child, stop running *AROUND*.
We're coming to the end of a long, long day.
Busy little child, this is no time to play.
You've got to settlc. You've got to settle.
You've got to settle *DOWN*.

Roll like a river, rock like the sea,
dream like a dreamer and come home to me.
I'm gonna rock you. Rock you to sleep.
I'm gonna rock you. Rock you to sleep.
To sleep—rock you to sleep.

Oh, little child, won't you settle *DOWN*?
Sweet little child, stop running *AROUND*.
The night sky's turning to a blue so deep.
Well, come on, little child, now it's time for sleep.
You've got to settle. You've got to settle.
Got to settle *DOWN*.

FOR MUSIC & ALL LYRICS,
PLEASE TURN TO PAGE 53

DOG TRAIN! RIDING ALL NIGHT LONG, ON THAT DOG TRAIN! THEY'LL BE RIDING TILL DAWN. YOU'LL NEVER EVER SEE IT AS IT ROCKETS PAST— THE TRAIN GOES NOWHERE, BUT IT GOES THERE *FAST*. DOG TRAIN!

PART TWO

SING AND PLAY ALONG

TRACK # 1 Tantrum

No.   I don't   want   to.   I don't   want   to.   No.   I   don't

want   to.   No   no.   No.   I don't   want   to.   I don't   want   to.

No,   no,   no.   I don't   want   to.   Oh   no.   Leave   me   a - lone.

I don't want to be quiet.
I don't want to be good.
I don't want to do anything
if you tell me I should.
I won't listen to you.
If you call, I won't come.
All I want to do now...is have a tantrum.

No no no, I don't want to, I don't want to.
No no no, I don't want to, no no.
No no no, I don't want to, I don't want to.
No no no, I don't want to, no no.
No no no, I don't want to, I don't want to.
No no no, I don't want to, no no.
Leave me alone. Leave me alone.
LEAVE ME ALO—NE!

I don't want to be QUIET.
I don't want to BE good.
And I won't cooperATE
if you tell me I should.
I don't want to beHAVE.
I won't go to MY room.
Gonna rant. Gonna RAVE.
Gonna throw a TANtrum. TAAAN-trum.

I'm a wild child,
and I'm gonna make a scene.
I'm a WILD CHILD!
Let me show you what I mean:

Now I'm down on the ground.
(Now I'm down on the ground.)

And I'm shaking my head.
(And I'm shaking my head.)

And I'm kicking my feet.
(And I'm kicking my feet.)

And I'm pounding the floor.
(And I'm kicking my feet and
I'm kicking my feet and
I'm kicking my feet and...)

Leave me alone.
Leave me alone.
Leave me alone.
Leave me alone.
Leave me alone.........

DON'T leave me alone!
DON'T leave me alone!
DON'T leave me alone!
DON'T leave me alone!

DON'T!

DON'TDON'TDON'T!

No no no, I don't want to, I don't want to.
No no no, I don't want to, no no.
No no no, I don't want to, I don't want to.
No no no, I don't want to, no no.
No no no, I don't want to, I don't want to.
No no no, I don't want to, no no.
Leave me alone.
DON'T
leave me alone!

Well I'm gonna be QUIET
and I'm gonna BE good
and I might cooperATE
if you tell me I should.
I've got something to SAY
and you never WILL guess:
If you ask the right WAY,
then I'm gonna say...

no.

Thus Quacked Zarathustra

TRACK #
3 Dog Train

CHORUS

Dog Train! Rid-ing all night long,__ on that Dog Train! They'll be rid-ing till dawn. You'll nev-er ev-er see it as it rock-ets__ past.__ The train goes no-where, but it goes there__ fast.__ Dog__ Train.

Along about midnight when it's
dark, dark, dark
there's a long, low whistle
and a faraway bark
and then a
high, high whistle
only hounds can hear
to let 'em know the train,
the Dog Train is near.

[CHORUS]
Now the dogs never know
when they'll be going at all.
They've gotta lie around home,
and wait for the call.
But it has to be warm
so the doggies can ride
with their ears in the breeze
and their noses outside.
Their cold, wet, happy,
quiv'ring noses outside.
They run away to get aboard the—

[CHORUS]
There are 7,000 dogs
in eighty-eight cars,
a sliver of moon
and millions of stars.
And every single dog has

only one need: to ride
this train at a dazzling speed.
Dog Train. DOG TRAAAIN!
Dog Train.

Kittycats are not allowed.
No, kittycats are not allowed.
No, kittycats don't want to ride
the Dog Train.
Kittycats are not allowed.
No, kittycats are not allowed.
No, kittycats won't go,
'cause it's a Dog Train.
(A cat would be a catastrophe.
A cat would be a catastrophe.)

Now what've we got?
Now what've we got?
Now what've we got?
Well, we've got:

Big dogs and little dogs
and right-smack-in-the-middle dogs
fat dogs and skinny dogs
and quite absurdly mini-dogs
city dogs and pretty dogs
from way out of town
dogs in every shade of black,

white, and brown
lumbering dogs
and doggies that spring
and one small fluffy pink
poodle-y thing
old dogs and new dogs
and fine dogs and true dogs and
sleek dogs and shaggy dogs and
DOGS, DOGS, DOGS, DOGS!

[CHORUS]
So fast. Dog Train.
Dog Traaaain!

What do you want to know about it?
What do you want to know about it?
What do you want to know about
the Dog Train?
What do you want to know about it?
What do you want to know about it?
What do you want to know about
the Dog Train?

It has to be warm
so the doggies can ride
with their ears in the breeze
and their noses outside.

Oooooooooooo…

Now if you notice that your dog
is just lazing around
with its head on its paws
and its tail on the ground,
well, by now you realize
there's a simple explanation:
chances are your dog has been
ALL OVER CREATION
on the—

[CHORUS]
When the whistle blows,
they all howl along—
It's their very own version
of the Dog Train song.
I wish I could travel with them
on that—

[CHORUS]
Think about it, Rover.
Choo-choo it over. Dog Train.
I wish I could travel with them
on that Dog Train.
Dog Train.
Doooooooog Train.

Hot diggitty dog, hot diggitty dog, hot diggitty
dog, hot diggitty dog, hot diggitty dog, hot
diggitty dog, hot diggitty dog, hot diggitty dog, hot
diggitty dog, hot diggitty dog, hot diggitty dog,
hot diggitty dog…

TRACK #
4

Sneakers

Well, I'm a big ol' bear, and I don't wear much of anything, 'cause I've got fur.
But these big ol' feet wouldn't be complete without my shoes. No sir.
I'm talkin' about **SNEAKERS.** Yeah.

My old sneak-ers are friends of mine.___ You can't trust a-ny shoes that shine.___

Some shoes pinch you,___ some shoes___ squeak. The on-ly shoes that I would choose are

shoes that___ sneak.___ I'm tell-ing you, my old sneak-ers are friends of mine.___

You can't trust a-ny shoes that shine.___ Some shoes pinch you, some shoes squeak. The

on - ly shoes that I would choose are shoes that___ sneak.

Whoa! Look at these guys!

Well, there's a toe that is torn
and the laces are worn
so I've added a section of string.
I'm not even sure
what color they were,
but now they're a little
of everything. Oh—[CHORUS]

Sneak...

Now I'm walking around
without any sound.
I'm a quiet ol' bear,
and shy.
When you're unaware
that a bear is there,
well, here's the reason why:
it's the **SNEAKERS.**

Now you know.

They'll try to get you to use
uncomfortable shoes
when you've got to look
nice and neat.
But most of the time
you'll notice that I'm
keeping these sneakers
on my feet. [CHORUS]

The only real alternative is—
Yup: bear feet.

5 Cow Planet

Another time. Another place. Somewhere far. Out in space.
Listen: "COWWWWWWW...PLANET. AH-OOM."
Who they are, we don't know. Now they call. We must go. Cow Planet.

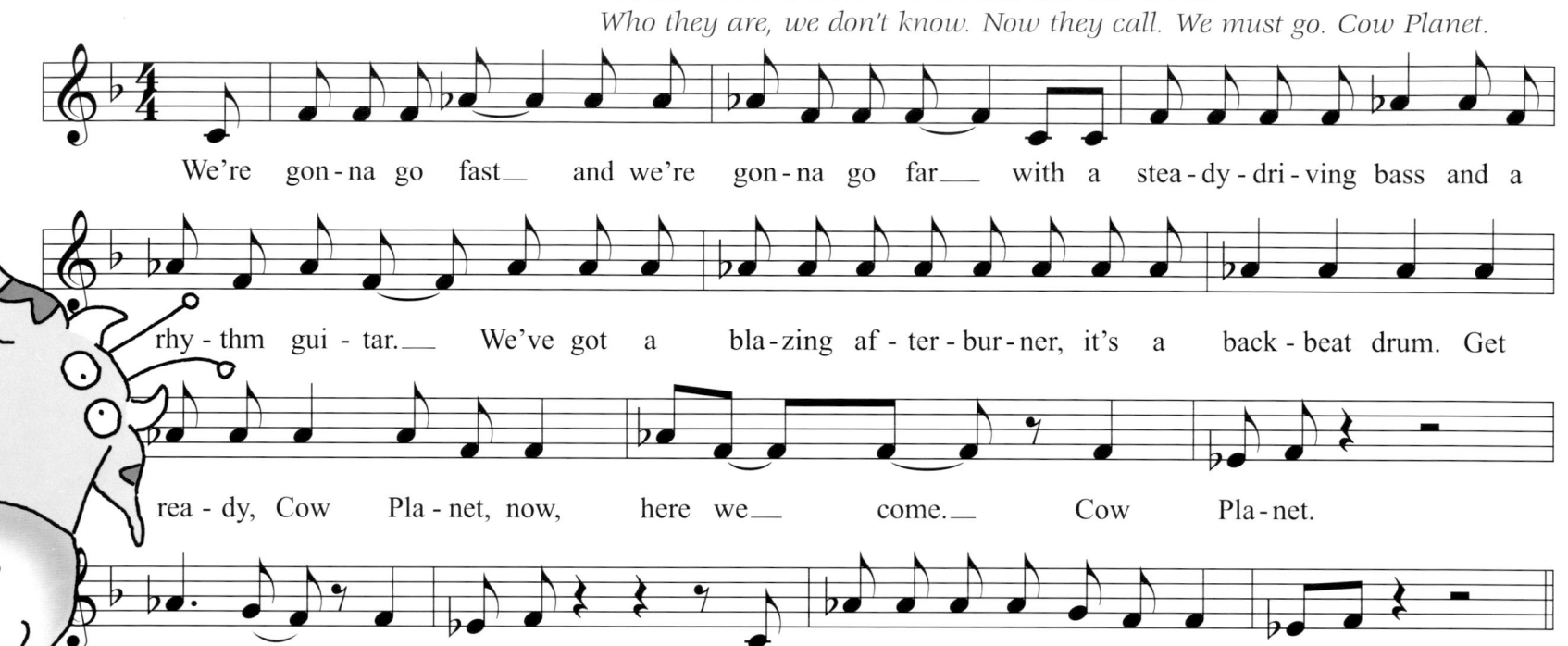

We're gon-na go fast___ and we're gon-na go far___ with a stea-dy-dri-ving bass and a rhy-thm gui-tar.___ We've got a bla-zing af-ter-bur-ner, it's a back-beat drum. Get rea-dy, Cow Pla-net, now, here we___ come.___ Cow Pla-net. Hey, hey,___ Cow Pla-net. We're real-ly on our way to Cow Pla-net.

MACH 1, MACH 2, OVERDRIVE, HYPERSPEED,
MAXIMUM VELOCITY...

Gravity releases.
We're in a small, silver rocket ship,
shooting through time. No sound.

"COWWWWWWW...PLANET." —Let's go!

We're gonna go fast
and we're gonna go far
with a steady-driving bass
and a rhythm guitar.
We've got a blazing afterburner —
it's a backbeat drum.
Get ready, Cow Planet, now, here we come.
Cow Planet. Whoa oh, Cow Planet.
We're really gonna go to Cow Planet.

Exactly where it is, well, we don't know yet,
but we're following the voices on our radio set.
And we'll keep on rock-and-rolling through outer space
till we find find find that magical place!

Cow Planet. Ohhhhh! Cow Planet.

YEAH!
We don't care if they're green.
We don't care if they're blue.
We just want them all to sing
in the way that they do.
And I'm telling you now:
just as soon as we land,
we're gonna add the cows
to our rock-and-roll band.

We're gonna add the cows
to our rock-and-roll band.
Yeah, we're gonna add the cows
to our rock-and-roll band!

Cow Planet. Hey, hey, Cow Planet.
Nothing else can say Cow Planet.
How can it? How can it?
We're really on our way to Cow Planet!
We're really on our way to Cow Planet!
We're really on our way to Cow Planet!

We will call the band "Mootopia."
It will be the greatest band ever.
Stay tuned. Cow Planet.
From deep space, over and out.

Boring Song

Suddenly here you are...

mmm____ right in the mid-dle of a bor-ing song.____ This song is so bor-ing, and

I'm____ bor-ing, too. Won't you let me be bor-ing,____ so bor-ing for you? And

though you find me bor-ing, still I'm a-dor-ing my voice. I've no choice. Yes, what

rit.

else can I do? It's im-pos-si-bly true. I'd give all that I've got just to tell of my love for me.____

Boring, boring, boring, boring...bo-ring, ooo!

TRACK # 7

Pots and Pans

CHORUS

I've got pots: Pots and pans._ I've got pots: Pots and pans._ Yeah,

that's the way_ that I like to play_ bang-ing on pots and pans._

Here we go.
I've got ONE pot.
A metal spoon.
What've you got?
You've got a rhythm tune.
You've got a pot. Spoon.
Rhythm tune.
You've got a pot
AND spoon AND
rhythm tune.
You've got a little,
got a lot, got a musical pot.
Now what? Now what?

[CHORUS]
Bangin' on pots and pans.

Now another pot.
A wooden spoon.
What've you got?
You've got a rhythm tune.
You've got a pot pot,
spoon spoon, rhythm tune.
You've got a 2-pot 2-spoon
2-2-tune.
You've got a little, got a lot,
got whatever you got.
Why not?
Ohhhh, yeah, why not?

[CHORUS]
Clangin' those pots and pans.

I'm so happy in the middle
of the kitchen floor...
with whatever I find
behind the cabinet door...
I don't want games
and I don't want toys—
just give me some things
that can make some noi-ZAH!

Give me pots.
[CHORUS]
Clangin' those pots and pans.
I'm sangin' about
pots and pans.

NOW I'M...KEEPING TIME...

Stop-look-listen to
what I've found.
I've got shimmer and shine
and collateral sound.
Hot! shimmer and shine
and collateral sound:
I've got copper pots...
and silver pans...
lots of lids...
and my garbage can.
Lids, can, pots, pans.
Playing it all with
my own two hands.
With a **JING ka DANG
WHAP! buh DAH dah BOOM!**

I can make enough racket
to rock the room!

[CHORUS]

I've got KNOCK-KNOCK-KNOCKING
on my door,
a lot of KNOCK-KNOCK-KNOCKING
on my door...
Come back later—
let me rock some more.
I said, come back later—
let me rock some more!
STOP that knocking,
I want to keep rocking.
STOP that knocking,
I want to keep rocking.
STOP that knocking,
I want to keep rocking.
But wait...
THAT'S GREAT!
Hey, hey! Don't go away!
Come on in so we can play.
Whoa! I've got one, two,
three, four calamity friends
coming through the door.
Let's play!

*We've got pots, pans,
and a rock-and-roll band.
We've got pots, pans,
and a rock-and-roll band.*

*Yeah, that's the way that
we like to play—
banging on pots and pans.
Banging on pots and pans.*

No, I don't need games
and I don't need toys—
Just give me those things
that can really make noise!

BLENDER SOLO!

We've got so much going
now, what do you think?
Might as well add the
kitchen sink! *Oooooo—
rock and roll, rolling and rocking.
Rock and roll, rolling and rocking.
Rock and roll, rolling and rocking.
That's the way that we
like to play—
banging on pots and pans.
Yeah, banging on pots and pans.*

When you've got something
that you want to say,
you're never gonna find
a superior way.
You've got to say it
with percussion.
End of discussion.
YUP! Done.

TRACK #
8

I Need a Nap

BOY
Well, the sun is still high in the afternoon sky,
but the morning seems so long ago.
I was happy before and I'm not any more,
though why there's a change, I don't know.

GIRL
I'm so tired of this day and I don't want to play
and I don't want a story to read.
But I look in your eyes and at once realize
that I know what it is...

BOY
Yes, I know what it is...
BOTH
Now I know what it is
that I need—

CHORUS

I need a nap! I just can't take a-ny more.

I need a nap! Can't stay a-wake a-ny more. No more

run - ning a - round I just need to lie down and sleep!

BOY
I don't know what to do.
I just can't make it through.
I want something,
or nothing, right now.

GIRL
I am mad and upset.
What I want, I don't get.
I don't know what I want anyhow.

BOY
I've been doing my best,
now I just want to rest—
on the rug, on the floor,
I don't care.

GIRL
Now the feeling's so strong,
but the song is too long—

it's the wrong kind of song—
and it seems to be going nowhere.

BOTH
Nowhere! Oh,

[CHORUS]

Let me sleeeeeeeeep!

There are times in your day
when the going gets tough,
when you just have to say
you've done more than enough.

BOY
I can't think of more stuff
that will rhyme with "enough"...

BOTH
So enough is enough...is enough
is enough...is enough is enough

is enough is enough is enough
is enough is...
I NEED A NAP!

BOY
Why does this song go on?

BOTH
I NEED A NAP!

BOY
When all my strength is gone?

BOTH
I NEED A NAP!

GIRL
Please let me close my eyes.

BOTH
I NEED A NAP!
I don't want to...harmonize!

With you!
With me!

BOY
Change keeeeeey!

GIRL
Make him stop.

BOTH
I NEED A NAP!
I just can't take any more.
I NEED A NAP!

BOY
Can't stay awake any more.

BOTH
You can follow my lead
as the song loses speed
now I need an immediate

NAAaaaaaaaaaaaa.............p.

Evermore

The for-ests of A - pril a - wa-ken from sleep, ___ and flow-ers un - fold through the

snow,   And the wind ru-shes_ high, and the riv-er_ runs deep, and it sings what you al-rea-dy know.

CHORUS

You al-rea-dy_ know.   Ev-er-more   I will love you. Ev-er - more I will stay   ev-er

right here to hold you. Nev-er so far a - way.   And   though I know some-times you go   to

find your way a - lone,_   ev-er-more I will love you. You are ev - er my   own.

Though nothing's as certain as seasons and time,
though nothing will be as before,
still every way and always it's certain that I'm
with you forever, evermore.

[CHORUS]

Ever my own. Ever my own.
Forever and evermore.

Penguin Lament

If you were a pen-guin, you'd un-der-stand how it is to be a pen-guin. It's not al-ways grand.

If you were a pen-guin, then you could tell what it's like to be a pen-guin. You'd know too

CHORUS

well. And I'm a lit-tle too cute. Oh, yes, I know. I'm all dressed up, but I've got no place to go.

When you are a penguin,
you look around
and see nothing but penguins
and frozen ground.

When you are a penguin—
and I am one—
you have nowhere to hide.
You have no way to run.

Little legs cannot stride
so we rock side to side,
side to side, side to side
to move.
We can't even fly!

[CHORUS]

I want to be cool,
like the polar bear guys.
I want to be tall
and somewhat mysterious.

But nothing profound
comes in penguin size.
Can anyone small...
be anyone serious?

I'M SERIOUS!

A little too cute.
A little too cute.
A little too cute.

[CHORUS]

Now, I am a penguin.

No one else like me.
Except every other penguin
that you ever will see.
MILES OF PENGUINS
as cute as can be.

We're all a little too cute.
Oh, yes, we know.
A little too cute,
Oh, yes, we know.
A little TOO cute,
Oh, yes, we know.
A little TOO cute,
Oh, yes, we know.
A little too cute,
Oh, yeah, that's right—
we're all dressed up,

*and we're gonna
have a party tonight!*

¡VÁMONOS, PINGUÍNOS!

*Penguin!
Penguin Party, now!
Ah! ah-ah—
Penguin! Penguin!
Penguin Party, now!*

I LOVE MY LIFE!

*You gotta
rock-and-roll it at a
Penguin!*

GO, JOHNNY, GO!

Penguin Party, now!

WHERE'D YOU GET THAT TUX?

TRACK #
12
(Don't Give Me That) Broccoli

Do - on't give me that broc-co - LEE.__ Uh-oh-oh. Do - on't give me that__   BROC-Co-li.__   Yes, I

know I've nev - er tried it, but it   does - n't look right.   I   want no broc-c'li to - night.__

Now listen, Nice Lady,
I don't want to be unfair,
and I know you try to
do your best.
I appreciate the fact
that you really do care,
but I have a
most important request.
Please listen, can you listen,
won't you listen to me?
I'd rather that you never
give me...broccoLEE.
Please. Don't don't give me
any broccoli.

Do-on't give me that
broccoLEE. Uh-oh-oh.
Do-on't give me that BROCColi.
You tell me it can't hurt me
to take one little bite, but I'm
taking no chances tonight.

You always try to tell me
that it's good for me,
if I want to grow up
big and strong.
But how can I eat something
that looks just like a tree?
That can't be right.
It has got to be wrong.
Oh! Don't give me that.
Oh! Don't give me that.
Oh! Don't give me that
B-R-O-C-C-O-L-I (ee-i-ee-i-ee-i...)

You know I'm not the
only one who feels this way.
The popularity of brocc'li
is low.
When people come to dinner,
if it's Broccoli Day, they say,
      "Thank you but we
         really must go."

You can hear it down in Texas—

   **"Darlin', I'm giving back
      the brockly you gave me..."**

You can hear it in Québec—

   **"Ne me donnez pas
      ces brocolis-là."**

You can hear it off in Italy, too—

   **"O, Broccoli miei,
      non vi amo..."**

Yeah, and even Cow Planet,
if you're very hi tech—

   "NOOO...BROCC'LI."

You can listen to me tell it to you—

Don't don't give me that broccoli!
Don't don't give me that broccoli!

Don't don't give me
that broccoli!

Oh,
pleeeeeeeeeease.
Not ever.
No never.
Never never ever ever
ever ever ever ever
ever ever...

Well okay,
I'm gonna try it
but it isn't
on my diet
and I know
I'm going to hate it.
Uh! Oh!.......
I ate it.

Yum.

Dragonfire

Dra-gon - fire. It burns so hot, it burns so bright. Dra-gon - fire. Dra-gon-

fire. It burns so bright, it burns so ve-ry hot. Dra-gon - fire. So small I am, so new-ly

made. With-in me, a flame to keep me__ un-a-fraid. Un - a - fraid. My__ Dra-gon - fire.

Dragonfire.
It burns so hot,
it burns so bright.
Dragonfire.

Dragonfire.
It burns so bright,
it burns so very hot.
Dragonfire.

Yeah,
yeah,
Dragonfire!

In the dark, Dragonfire.
In the cold, Dragonfire.
In the dark,
in the cold,
there's a spark
that I hold
here within me,
my own Dragonfire.
Dragonfire! Dragonfire!
Hey, Dragonfire!
Come, Dragonfire!
Dragonfire! I am
Dragonfire! Dragonfire.

Dragonfire.
It burns so hot,
it burns so bright.
It burns so pure.
Dragonfire.

So small I am,
so newly made.
Within me, a flame
to keep me unafraid.
Most unafraid.
Ever unafraid.
Dragonfire.

I am small, but complete.
I have light. I have heat.
I am never alone.
I can summon my own
Dragonfire! Dragonfire!
Dragonfire!

Hey, Dragonfire.
Dragonfire.
Dragonfire.

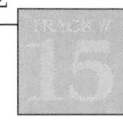

Wave Bye-Bye

Excuse me, please...Mommy?...Excuse me, please...I want to go.

Well, hey hey___ pret-ty Mom-my, can you hear me at all? There's lots of noi-sy peo-ple and they're

way too__ tall.   I don't want to hear that mu-sic. I don't like the food.___ It's e - nough to put a child in a

ve-ry bad mood.   Come on and say bye - bye.   I want to   go bye - bye.   It's time to wave bye - bye.

Wave bye-bye.
There's a lot of conversation
going on and on.
If we never get going,
then we won't be gone.
They said it was a mistake,
but they made a mistake.
How can it be a party,
when there isn't a cake?

Yeah.

Come on and say bye-bye.
I want to go bye-bye.
It's time to wave bye-bye.
Wave bye-bye.

Sweet Daddy, can we please
get away from the crowd?
There are SO many people
and they laugh too loud.
I want them not to see me,
'cause whenever they do,
they've always got to ask me,
"And how old are you?" Well, huh.

Well, I was four when we got here.
It's a while since then.

I'm thinking that by now I must be...nine or ten.

Come on and say bye-bye. I want to go bye-bye.
It's time to wave bye-bye: Bye-bye.
Can't you feel me tugging on your jacket sleeve?
I'm very very tired and it's—time to leave!
Come on and say bye-bye. I want to go bye-bye.
It's time to wave bye-bye. Wave bye-bye.

Whenever it looks like we're about to go,
you suddenly notice someone else you know.
Can you tell me how much longer
I'm supposed to wait? It's late. Late.
It's almost eight!

Come on and say bye-bye. I want to go bye-bye.
It's time to wave bye-bye: Bye-bye.
They said it was a party. Big mistake.
How can it be a party, when they
DON'T HAVE CAKE?
Come on and say bye-bye. I want to go bye-bye.
It's time to wave bye-bye.
You've got to wave bye-bye.

Oh no.

Does anybody hear me? Does anybody care?
If you hear me, anybody, put your hands
in the air. That's right. Now wave.

Let's wave, yeah.
Wave them high: Bye-bye.
Wave them low: I gotta go.
Wave them left.
Wave them right.
THANKYOUVERYMUCH!
GOODBYE!GOODNIGHT!
Ah-huh. Oh, yeah.
Wave AND wave AND
wave some more.
Keep on waving.
We're out the door.
So nice. Okay.
Goodbye, Big People,
yeah that's the way.
Bye-bye. Just wave.
We're going home.
Bye-bye.   No ice cream.
Say goodbye.   No balloons.
Wave bye-bye.   No presents.
Bye-bye.   No piñata.
Bye-bye.   Some party.
Goodbye, Big People.
Wave bye-bye.
Just say goodbye.

No clown.

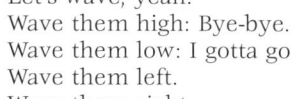

Rock to Sleep 54

Oh, little child, won't you settle DOWN?
Oh, little child, stop running AROUND.
We're coming to the end of
a long, long day.
Busy little child, this is no time to play.
You've got to settle. You've got to settle.
You've got to settle DOWN.

Roll like a riv-er, rock like the sea. Dream like a dream-er and come home to me. I'm gon-na rock you. Rock you to sleep. I'm gon-na rock you. Rock you to sleep._ To sleep. Rock you to sleep.

Oh, little child,
won't you settle DOWN?
Sweet little child,
stop running AROUND.
The night sky's turning
to a blue so deep.
Well, come on, little child,
now it's—time for sleep.
You've got to settle.
You've got to settle.
Got to settle DOWN.

Roll like a river,
rock like the sea.
Dream like a dreamer
and come home to me. To me.
I'm gonna rock you.
Rock you to sleep.
I'm gonna rock you.
Rock you to sleep.
I'm gonna rock you, rock you,
rock you to sleep.
Oh, little child. Oh, little child.

Roll like a river.
Like a river.
Rock like the sea.
Like the sea.
Dream like a dreamer.
Dream like a dreamer.
Come home.
Now I rock you.
Rock you to sleep.
rock you...

to sleep...
rock you...
star child...
hush...
rock you...
Rock you to
sleep...
Dream away.

Away!

PART THREE

ABOUT THE ARTISTS

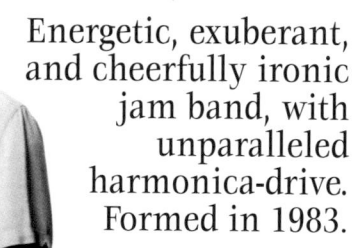

SPIN DOCTORS

Good-natured, inventive jam band, formed in 1988, disbanded in 1996, reunited in 2001.

CHRIS BARRON vocals
AARON COMESS drums
MARK WHITE bass
ERIC SCHENKMAN guitar

Best known for

album POCKET FULL OF KRYPTONITE, and singles *Two Princes* and *Little Miss Can't Be Wrong*.

WEBSITE: www.spindoctors.com

PAUL LA RAIA

SANDRA BOYNTON

BLUES TRAVELER

THE O.K. CHORALE

Feisty and fictitious choral ensemble, made up of enthusiastic farm animals of startling musicianship.

TAD KINCHLA bass
BRENDAN HILL drums
CHAN KINCHLA guitar
JOHN POPPER
 vocals & harmonicas
BEN WILSON piano

WEBSITE: www.bluestraveler.com

Energetic, exuberant, and cheerfully ironic jam band, with unparalleled harmonica-drive. Formed in 1983.

Best known for

album FOUR, and singles *Hook* and *Run Around* (Grammy® winner, and the longest-charting single in Billboard history)

PAUL BROWN

MARK LANEGAN

Evocative, infinitely cool singer and songwriter, much sought after for his distinctive low-down voice, and his remarkable vocal and stylistic range.

WEBSITE: www.marklanegan.com

STEVE GULLICK

Best known for

fronting the influential Seattle band, The Screaming Trees (formed 1984), The Mark Lanegan Band, and guest vocals for Queens of the Stone Age

STEVE LAWRENCE & EYDIE GORME

(on the right)   (on the left)

Separately and together, two of the truly great classic American singers, recording and performing continuously since the mid-1950s.

Best known for

pretty much everything. They have Top Ten hits, they have Grammys® , they have Emmys®, they have two major lifetime achievement awards. They've also done a terrific cover of Soundgarden's *Black Hole Sun*. Honest.

WEBSITE: www.steveandeydie.com

BILLY J. KRAMER

Charismatic British Invasion Merseybeat singer, discovered and signed by Brian Epstein in 1962, and (backed up by The Dakotas) produced by George Martin at Abbey Road.

Best known for

singles *Do You Want to Know a Secret?*, *Bad to Me* (both Lennon/McCartney), and *Little Children*

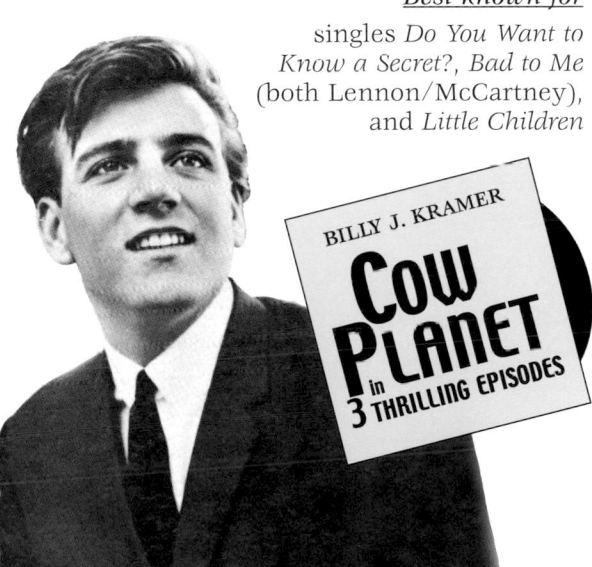

WEBSITE: www.billyjkramer.com

THE BACON BROTHERS

TIMOTHY WHITE

KEVIN BACON vocals
MICHAEL BACON vocals & guitar

Wry and eclectic duo, skillfully traveling intertwining paths of folk, rock, soul, and country (hence the title of their nifty 1997 debut album, FOROSOCO).

Best known for

singing *Guess Again*, *Woman's Got a Mind to Change*, and *Footloose.* (And, of course, *Philadelphia Chickens.*) Michael also scores films, and Kevin is zero degrees away from Kevin Bacon.

WEBSITE: www.baconbros.com

POTS AND PANS
THE BACON BROTHERS and MICKEY HART

MICKEY HART

Complex percussionist, solo artist, and noted authority on world music traditions.

Best known for

longtime drummer/percussionist for the Grateful Dead (starting in 1967) and Grammy® winner for his 1991 album, PLANET DRUM

WEBSITE: www.mickeyhart.net

JOHN WERNER

KATE WINSLET

"WEIRD AL" YANKOVIC

I NEED
A NAP!
KATE WINSLET &
"WEIRD AL" YANKOVIC

JASON BELL

WEBSITE: www.weirdal.com

MARK SELIGER

Spirited and captivating British
actress, much admired for her
artistic independence, her
bold and nuanced characters,
and her true versatility.

Absurdly brilliant parodist,
and the bestselling comedy artist ever,
since 1979 satirizing American pop culture
in virtuosic, oddly profound songs
and wildly innovative videos.

Best known for

many films, including *Sense and Sensibility,
Titanic,* and *Eternal Sunshine of the Spotless Mind.*
Four Oscar® and four Golden Globe® nominations,
all before the age of 30.

Best known for

lots of albums and manymanymany singles,
including *Smells Like Nirvana* and *Amish Paradise,*
and the cult classic movie *"UHF."*
And three Grammys® (nine nominations).

This is Ms. Winslet and Mr. Yankovic's first duet together.

RUSS HARRINGTON

ALISON KRAUSS

Revered bluegrass musician and record producer, noted for her exquisite vocals and astonishing fiddle playing. Since the release of her first album in 1987 (she was 16), Alison has recorded and toured extensively with her superb longtime band, Union Station.

Best known for many albums, and many singles including _The Lucky One, Forget About It, Now That I've Found You_, and the Beatles' _I Will_. And a record-breaking 17 Grammys®.

WEBSITE: www.alisonkrauss.com

Evermore

ALISON KRAUSS

PENGUIN LAMENT

JOHN ONDRASIK _of_ FIVE FOR FIGHTING

JIM WRIGHT

THE PHENOMENAUTS

CORPORAL JOEBOT V 2.0 lead vocals & guitar
COMMANDER ANGEL NOVA harmonies & guitar
MAJOR JIMMY BOOM drums
CAPTAIN CHREEHOS MAAS upright bass
PROFESSOR GREG ARIUS keyboards
COL. REEHOTCH M.O.S.

Since 2000, San Francisco's own irrepressible 50s space-themed rocket rollers. Guided by the motto "Science and Honor," they have inspired a loyal following of Earth people who want less cynicism and more celebration.

Best known for

commando-style street performances, and their rousing single, _Earth Is the Best_

WEBSITE: www.phenomenauts.com

LIZ LAZICH

(Don't Give Me That) BROCCOLI
THE PHENOMENAUTS

JOHN ONDRASIK _of_ FIVE FOR FIGHTING

Iconoclastic, reflective, intense singer/songwriter/guitarist/pianist/chess prodigy/sportswriter (who pretty much IS Five For Fighting).

Best known for

singles _Superman (It's Not Easy)_ and _100 Years_, albums MESSAGE FOR ALBERT, AMERICA TOWN, and THE BATTLE FOR EVERYTHING

WEBSITE: www.fiveforfighting.com

Wave Bye-Bye
DOSHIE LUTHER

RICK WHITEHEAD

WEBSITE:
www.hadassahtoday.com

DOSHIE LUTHER

Powerful and brightly attitudinal down-home singer, performing nationwide for the past 12 years. She's now 18. Doshie is also a national spokesperson for the Children's Rights Council.

ROB HYMAN & ERIC BAZILIAN
(on the right)   (on the left)

ROB HYMAN lead vocals, melodica, synth
ERIC BAZILIAN harmonies, guitar, mandolin, recorder

Terrific rockers, songwriters, record producers. Cofounders (in 1980) of Philadelphia's famed melodic rock band, The Hooters.

Best known for
album NERVOUS NIGHT with three hit singles *Day by Day, And We Danced,* and *Where Do the Children Go?* Eric wrote Grammy® winner *One of Us,* sung by Joan Osborne. Rob wrote and performed *Time After Time* with Cyndi Lauper.

ROB HYMAN & ERIC BAZILIAN
DRAGONFIRE

JOHN GRAHAM / GRAHAM STUDIOS

WEBSITE:
www.thehooters.net

Rock to Sleep 54
HOOTIE & THE BLOWFISH

MARK TUCKER

HOOTIE & THE BLOWFISH

JIM "SONI" SONEFELD drums, harmonies
MARK BRYAN guitar
DARIUS RUCKER vocals
DEAN FELBER bass, harmonies

Fine and friendly Southern Rock band, with always a little heartfelt smokiness.

Best known for

their HUGELY popular debut album, *Cracked Rear View* (1994) with three hit singles *Hold My Hand, Let Her Cry,* and *Only Wanna Be With You.*

WEBSITE: www.hootie.com

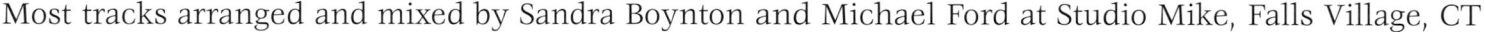

Recording Credits

Please see CD insert on page 65 for track-by-track detail.

PRODUCED BY SANDRA BOYNTON
& MICHAEL FORD

Most tracks arranged and mixed by Sandra Boynton and Michael Ford at Studio Mike, Falls Village, CT

Dog Train mixed by the fabulous CHRIS TERGESEN at Hit Factory, NYC • assistant engineer Jon Belec
Evermore mixed by the also fabulous GARY PACZOZA at Minutia Sound, Nashville, TN

Mastered by the legendary CHRIS GEHRINGER at Sterling Sound, NYC
assistant engineer WILL QUINNELL

Lyrics by Sandra Boynton • Music by—

Tantrum BOYNTON
Thus Quacked Zarathustra STRAUSS
Dog Train BOYNTON
Sneakers BOYNTON
Cow Planet BOYNTON
Boring Song BOYNTON/FORD
Pots and Pans BOYNTON

I Need a Nap BOYNTON
Evermore BOYNTON/FORD
Penguin Lament BOYNTON
(Don't Give Me That) Broccoli BOYNTON
Dragonfire BOYNTON
Wave Bye-Bye BOYNTON
Rock to Sleep 54 BOYNTON

Michael Ford plays keyboards and/or piano on tracks # 1, 2, 3, 4, 5, 6, 7, 8, 9, 10, 11, 12, 14 & 15
and Wurlitzer piano on tracks 11 & 16.

Sandra Boynton had to pretty much make all the coffee entirely by herself.

Spin Doctors appear courtesy of Ruffnation Music
Blues Traveler appears courtesy of Vanguard Records
The Bacon Brothers appear courtesy of Forosoco Records
Al Yankovic appears courtesy of Volcano Records
Alison Krauss appears courtesy of Rounder Records
John Ondrasik of Five For Fighting appears courtesy of Aware/Columbia Records
The Phenomenauts appear courtesy of Springman Records
Hootie & the Blowfish appear courtesy of Sneaky Long Records

& Thank-yous

TO **JAMIE McEWAN**
my so-very-adored traveling companion —*Sandy*

TO **BETH ANDRIEN**
forever my source of inspiration —*Mike*

CAITLIN, KEITH, DEVIN & DARCY
and **RACHEL, JOHN & KATIE**
for their loving support
throughout our adventure

KATHLEEN T. SHERRILL
for stabilization around sharp curves
(and remember, K.T.—
the L.A. traffic is really really terrible)

TO FINE FAMILY & GOOD FRIENDS
[from SB:]
of course Mike and Beth
Jeanne Boynton, Jacquelyn Tintle
Dara & Linda Epstein, David Allender
Robin Corey, Sarah Getz, the Keisers, the Kirbers
the Manns, the Ortolanis, Susan Spano
the Stanleys, the Workmans, Sheila Hough
Ken Chase, Jay d'Andrea, Gina & Bruce Young
[from SB & MF:]
the Biaginis, Pam Boynton & John Stey
all Boyntons & McEwans everywhere
Randy Dwenger & Steve Callahan
the Capecclatros, the Clarkes
Frank Grusauskas, all the Heaths, Laura Linney
Doshie & Betty Jo Luther, Keturah Murnane
Suzanne Rafer & Danny Peary, Nora & Bob Rivkin
Christine Stevens, Chris Tergesen & Toni Lewis
[from MF:]
Pat & Marlene, Lucyann & John
the Andriens, Elsie Finnerty, Noel Heagerty
Jess Ricciardi, Carl Kusnell, Steve Black
my Adam's Mark Family
John Senior & Nancy Kimmons
Dick Lolla & Paula Pierce
and again to Rachel, for holding down the home fort

"Sandy, your Dragonfire burns incredibly bright. Thank you for
sharing its warmth, and illuminating a pathway back to our childhood."

STEADY VIDEOGRAPHER & INSIGHTFUL MUSE Beth Andrien
SUPERB A & R CONSULTATION Devin McEwan
WONDERFUL MUSIC BIZ GUIDANCE Jay Levey, Scott McGhee
SKILLFULLY TURNING TWO DIMENSIONS INTO THREE Terry Ortolani

TERRIFIC DEMO PERFORMANCE
Beth Andrien, Darcy Boynton, Keith Boynton, Caitlin McEwan
Michaela Romano-Meade, Graham Stone, Adam Riccio, Rob Tawse

ATTENTIVE ARTIST MANAGEMENT
Scott McGhee, Terry Bleckley of McGhee Entertainment
Jay Levey of Imaginary Entmt. • Carla Sacks of Sacks & Co.
Jim Grant of Little Big Man • Judy Tannen of G.L. Music
Jennifer Templeton, Denise Stiff of DS Management
John Dee, Kevin Gasser, Casey Brown of Benchmark Entmt.
William Derella, Jason Richardson of DAS Communications
Steve Mountain, Chris McNelis of Cornerstone Mgmt.
Jared Paul of azoff music, Marc Tamo of Fat Wreck Chords
Roger Skelton at Volcano • Susan Jacobs at Sony
Jamie Kitman at The Hornblow Group

CHEERFUL AND EFFICIENT LOGISTICAL HELP
Susan Mieras, Gina Z, Colin Speir, Col. Reehotch (Rich)
Mark & Laura Bryan, Caryl Hart, Mary Ann Wade
Janine Gray, Stacey Adamski, Sam Mendes
R. Mahoney, F. Essenfeld, D. Petrafesa & O. Arredondo of BT
Lauren Caracciolo at Merrill Lynch, Ivy Koral at ICM
Kurt Soto of Vans Warped Tour, Caryl McGowan at Sterling Sound
the wonderful people at the St. Regis Hotel, NYC
Matt Micucci and all at Shutters, Santa Monica
Cecil and all at Gruene Mansion, Texas
Lisa Hoage & Jill Thomen at the post office

ALL THESE GREAT MUSIC PEOPLE
Mark Bruhn at Sweetwater Sound
Paul at Ironwood • Christine Zoro/WKZE
K.C. & Aimee Porter at World Beat Recording
Zoë Thrall at Hit Factory • Tino Passante at Avatar
Buddy Brundo, Lisa Stuck at Conway • Lisa Zahn at NARAS
Mary Ellen Bernard at Triple Z • all at DB Digital Plus

CONVEYORS OF THOUGHTFUL ENTHUSIASM
AT CRITICAL JUNCTURES Jean Schulz, John Ondrasik
Mark Linn-Baker, Skip Strobel, Chandler Kinchla
Cary Sherman, Al & Suzanne Yankovic, Sergio d'Ercole
Roni & William Ashton (a.k.a. Billy J. Kramer), Chris Shiflett
Delana Gardner, Hy Lit, Matt Hanks, Viktor & Kristi Krauss
Bertis Downs, Bruce Flohr, Michael Meisel, Niels Schroeter

Book Credits & Thank-yous

My profound admiration and appreciation go to the diligent and agreeable crew at Workman Publishing, who have made this journey so pleasant and worthwhile:

EDITOR/STATIONMASTER (night shift *and* day shift) **Suzanne Rafer**

STREAMLINING **Paul Hanson**

PRE-PRODUCTION/LAYING THE RAILS
Harry Schroder
with **Sue Macleod, Philip Hoffhines**

SAnDrA

BOLD & EFFICIENT PRODUCTION **Wayne Kirn, Sarah Henry**

FIRST CLASS MARKETING
Katie Workman
with **Pete Bohan, Leda Marritz & David Schiller**

PUBLICITY/LOCOMOTION **Kim Small and Kim Hicks**

PRODUCTION EDITOR **Mary Ann McLaughlin**

THE MUSIC GUY **Bruce Johnson**

THE BENEVOLENT TYCOON **Peter Workman**

The beautiful farm painting on the wall of page 34 is by renowned Vermont landscape artist, Eric Tobin (artist@pshift.com)

And thank you once again to the wonderful folks at Novellus Graphics, Toronto
RON, SHAWN AND MICHAEL RICKETTS, CHRISTINE ANTONSEN, WAYNE BOOTH, ANDREW BENT, AND DAVID MCMULLEN
for their cheerful attention to the complexities of art reproduction.

Free!
Do-it-yourself CD Case Insert!

FOLD→

If you find that your CD wants to get out a little, maybe see the world, yet your book prefers to laze around the house, you could make a spiffy travel case for your DOG TRAIN Compact Disc. Simply cut where indicated, then fold the 2 side flaps inward, and now you're ready to ooch this handy and informative insert into a new clear plastic case. Or maybe just use the case of some old CD that doesn't really meet your family's needs at this particular point in time.

FOLD→

CUT HERE
VERTICALLY

1. **Tantrum** [3:12]
THE SPIN DOCTORS
recorded at AVATAR STUDIOS, NYC
Recording Engineer CHRIS THEGESEN
Assistant Engineer AYA TAKEMURA

2. **Thus Quacked Zarathustra**
[0:40] THE O. K. CHORALE
(AND GUEST AARDVARKS)
KEITH BOYNTON   TIM HAHN
MICHAEL FORD   MARK LINN-BAKER
JAMES CRESQUE   DEVIN McEWAN
KATIE FORD
recorded at STUDIO MIKE, FALLS MT., CT
Recording Engineer MICHAEL FORD

3. **Dog Train** [4:35]
BLUES TRAVELER
recorded at IRONWOOD STUDIOS, SEATTLE
Recording Engineers
CHRIS THEGESEN & DONN DEVORE
Assistant Engineer OWEN STRAUN
intern HIRA NAKAGAWA

4. **Sneakers** [2:23]
MARK LANEGAN
recorded at CONWAY STUDIOS, L.A.
Recording Engineer JOSHUA BLANCHARD
Assistant Engineer SAM HOLLAND

5. **Cow Planet** [3:46]
BILLY J. KRAMER
additional stuff by MF & SB

6. **Boring Song** [1:29]
STEVE LAWRENCE &
EYDIE GORME
with TOM FONTROSSES
recorded at SONY STUDIOS, NYC
Recording Engineer DON SWOPE
Assistant Engineer VAL BRAITHWAITE

7. **Pots and Pans** [3:21]
THE BACON BROTHERS
recorded at 4TH ST. RECORDING, SANTA MONICA
Recording Engineer CHRIS THEGESEN
Assistant Engineer NATE HERTWECK

PAUL GUZZONE bass & back-up vocals
GRAHAM STONE backup vocals
add'l percussion/general chaos: MF & SB
recorded at TRIPLE 2 STUDIO, BROOKLYN, NY
Recording Engineer PAUL GUZZONE

MICKEY HART
recorded at MICKEY HART'S PLACE
Northern CA
Recording Engineer RICHARD FISHER

8. **I Need a Nap** [3:35]
"WEIRD AL" YANKOVIC
recorded at RECORD ONE, L.A.
Recording Engineer CHRIS THEGESEN
Assistant Engineer BRIAN VIBBERTS

KATE WINSLET
recorded at STUDIO MIKE, FALLS MT., CT
Recording Engineer MICHAEL FORD

9. **Evermore** [3:11]
ALISON KRAUSS
RON BLOCK guitar
VICTOR KRAUSS bass
LARRY ATAMANICK drums
MICHAEL FORD piano
recorded at EMERALD STUDIOS, NASHVILLE
Recording Engineer GARY PACZOSA
Additional engineering BRANDON BELL

10. **Cow Planet** EPISODE 2 [1:18]
BILLY J. KRAMER
supporting cast
BETH ANDRIEN, MF & SB

11. **Penguin Lament** [3:32]
JOHN ONDRASIK of
FIVE FOR FIGHTING
back-up vocals
KEITH BOYNTON & GRAHAM STONE
recorded at WORLD BEAT PRODUCTIONS
WOODLAND HILLS, CA
Recording Engineer CHRIS THEGESEN
Assistant Engineer ALFONSO RODENAS

12. (Don't Give Me That) **Broccoli**
[2:25] THE PHENOMENAUTS
cellists
MICHAEL TEX FORD, LES QUIEBOOIS,
MICHAEL ENRICO FORD, C. P. COWS
recorded at WESTLAKE AUDIO, L.A.
Assistant Engineer JOHN ADAMS

13. **Dragonfire** [3:38]
ERIC BAZILIAN and ROB HYMAN
recorded at ELM STREET STUDIO, PHILADELPHIA
Recording Engineer JOHN SENIOR

14. **Cow Planet** EPISODE 3 [1:54]
BILLY J. KRAMER and MOOTOPIA
KEITH BOYNTON as ROD LEISTER

15. **Wave Bye-Bye** [3:15]
DOSHIE LUTHER
party guests: BETH, MIKE, SANDY,
and KATHLEEN "ETTA" SHERRILL
recorded at STUDIO MIKE, FALLS MT., CT
Recording Engineer MICHAEL FORD

16. **Rock to Sleep 54** [2:56]
HOOTIE & THE BLOWFISH
MICHAEL FORD Wurlitzer piano
recorded at MARK BRYAN'S PLACE
CHARLESTON, SC
Recording Engineer MIKE CORTAZZO

17. **Dog Train Midnight Jam**
(instrumental) [2:10]
BRENDAN HILL drums
JOHN POPPER harmonicas

TOTAL PROGRAM 47:54

THANK YOU! THANK YOU!

TO
JAMIE McEWAN
my so-very-adored traveling companion — *Sandy*

BETH ANDRIEN
forever my source of inspiration — *Mike*

CAITLIN, KEITH, DEVIN
and **RACHEL, JOHN & KATIE**
for their loving support throughout our adventure

KATHLEEN T. SHERRILL
for stabilization around sharp curves
(and remember, K.T.—the L.A. traffic is really really terrible)

TO FINE FAMILY & GOOD FRIENDS

[from SB:]
of course Mike and Beth
Jeanne Boynton, Jacquelyn Tintle, Dara & Linda Epstein
David Allender, Robin Corey, Sarah Getz
the Keisers, the Kirbers, the Manns, the Ortolanis
Susan Spano, the Stanleys, the Workmans, Sheila Hough
Ken Chase, Jay d'Andrea, Gina & Bruce Young

[from SB & MF:]
the Biaginis, Pam Boynton & John Stey
all Boyntons & McEwans everywhere
Randy Dwenger & Steve Callahan
the Capecelatros, the Clarkes
Frank Grusauskas, all the Heaths, Laura Linney
Doshie & Betty Jo Luther, Keturah Murnane
Suzanne Rafer & Danny Peary, Nora & Bob Rivkin
Christine Stevens, Chris Tergesen & Toni Lewis

[from MF:]
Pat & Marlene, Lucyann & John
the Andriens, Elsie Finnerty, Noel Heagerty
Jess Ricciardi, Carl Kusmell, Steve Black
my Adam's Mark Family
John Senior & Nancy Kimmons
Dick Lolla & Paula Pierce
and again to Rachel, for holding down the home fort

STEADY VIDEOGRAPHER & INSIGHTFUL MUSE Beth Andrien
SUPERB A & R CONSULTATION Devin McEwan
WONDERFUL MUSIC BIZ GUIDANCE Jay Levey, Scott McGhee
SKILLFULLY TURNING TWO DIMENSIONS INTO THREE Terry Ortolani

TERRIFIC DEMO PERFORMANCE
Beth Andrien, Darcy Boynton, Keith Boynton, Caitlin McEwan
Michaela Romano-Meade, Graham Stone, Adam Riccio, Rob Tawse

ATTENTIVE ARTIST MANAGEMENT
Scott McGhee, Terry Bleckley of McGhee Entertainment
Jay Levey of Imaginary Entm'. • Matt Hanks at Shorefire
Jim Grant of Little Big Man • Judy Tannen of G.L. Music
Jennifer Templeton, Denise Stiff of DS Management
John Dee, Kevin Gasser, Casey Brown of Benchmark Entm't.
William Derella, Jason Richardson of DAS Communications
Steve Mountain, Chris McNelis of Cornerstone Mgmt.
Jared Paul of azoff music, Marc Tarno of Fat Wreck Chords
Roger Skelton at Volcano • Susan Jacobs at Sony
Jamie Kitman at The Hornblow Group

CHEERFUL AND EFFICIENT LOGISTICAL HELP
Susan Mieras, Gina Z, Colin Speir, Col. Reehoth (Rich)
Mark & Laura Bryan, Caryl Hart, Mary Ann Wade
Janine Gray, Stacey Adamski, Sam Mendes
R. Mahoney, F. Essenfeld, D. Petrafesa & O. Arredondo of BT
Lauren Caracciolo at Merrill Lynch, Ivy Koral at ICM
Kurt Soto of the Vans Warped Tour
the wonderful people at the St. Regis Hotel, NYC
Matt Micucci and all at Shutters, Santa Monica
Cecil and all at Gruene Mansion, Texas
Lisa Hoage & Jill Thomen at the post office

ALL THESE GREAT MUSIC PEOPLE
Mark Bruhn at Sweetwater, Caryl McGowan at Sterling Sound
Paul at Ironwood • Christine Zoro/WKZE
K.C. & Aimee Porter at World Beat Recording
Zoë Thrall at Hit Factory • Tino Passante at Avatar
Buddy Brundo, Lisa Stuck at Conway • Lisa Zahn at NARAS
Mary Ellen Bernard at Triple Z • all at DB Digital Plus

CONVEYORS OF THOUGHTFUL ENTHUSIASM AT CRITICAL JUNCTURES
John Ondrasik, Mark Linn-Baker, Skip Strobel, Jean Schulz
Al & Suzanne Yankovic, Roni & William Ashton (a.k.a. Billy J. Kramer)
Chandler Kinchla, Cary Sherman, Chris Shiflett, Delana Gardner
Hy Lit, Matt Hanks, Sergio d'Ercole, Viktor & Kristi Krauss
Bertis Downs, Bruce Flohr, Michael Meisel, Niels Schroeter

Boynton! recordings

Most tracks arranged & mixed by
Sandra Boynton and Michael Ford
at Studio Mike, Falls Village, CT

Dog Train mixed by Chris Tergesen
at Hit Factory, NYC

Evermore mixed by Gary Paczoza
at Minutia Sound, Nashville

Album mastered by the legendary
Chris Gehringer at Sterling Sound, NYC

PRODUCED BY
SANDRA BOYNTON
& MICHAEL FORD

Music by—

Tantrum Boynton
Thus Quacked Zarathustra Strauss
Dog Train Boynton
Sneakers Boynton
Cow Planet Boynton
Boring Song Boynton/Ford
Pots and Pans Boynton
I Need a Nap Boynton
Evermore Boynton/Ford
Penguin Lament Boynton
(Don't Give Me That) Broccoli Boynton
Dragonfire Boynton
Wave Bye-Bye Boynton
Rock to Sleep 54 Boynton

All lyrics by Sandra Boynton

Michael Ford plays keyboards and/or piano
on tracks # 1, 2, 3, 4, 5, 6, 7, 8, 9, 10, 11, 12,
14, & 15, and Wurlitzer piano on tracks 11 & 16.

Sandra Boynton had to pretty much
make all the coffee entirely by herself.

Spin Doctors appear courtesy of Ruffnation Music
Blues Traveler appears courtesy of Vanguard Records
Eric Stefani appears courtesy of Fressco Records
"Weird Al" Yankovic appears courtesy of Volcano Records
Allison Krauss appears courtesy of Rounder Records
The Persuasions appear courtesy of Springman Records
John Ondrasik appears courtesy of Aware/Columbia Records
The Bacon Brothers appear courtesy of Hunnypot Records
Hootie & the Blowfish appear courtesy of Sneaky Long Records